DISCOVER
KAUAI
The Garden Isle

Text by
STU DAWRS

Photographs by
ANN CECIL

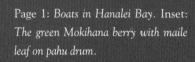

Page 1: *Boats in Hanalei Bay.* Inset: *The green Mokihana berry with maile leaf on pahu drum.*

This page, clockwise from top left: *Hā'ena Beach. Young Kahiko style hula dancer. Red Hibiscus. Ni'ihau Shell Leis. Motion of the hula. Hanalei beneath the mountains. Island faces from Kalāheo. Lobster claw heliconia.*

Opposite, clockwise from top left: *Golfer Ben Crenshaw. The Nā Pali Coast. Kahiko hula dancer. Pink Plumeria. Wailua Falls. A fisherman gathers his net. Lei display. Sunset at Po'ipū Beach.*

Center: *Hula dancer.*

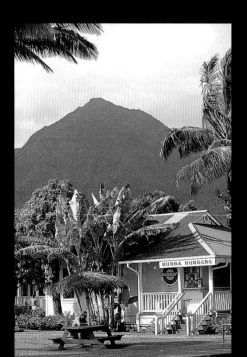

CONTENTS

E KOMO MAI

WELCOME!

KAUA'I HAS ALWAYS BEEN AN ISLAND APART. Lush, verdant and, well, wet—Mount Wai'ale'ale, the second highest point on the island, is the wettest spot on earth—the island is crisscrossed with rivers, streams and waterfalls, which is why it is popularly known as the Garden Island. Full of legend and as much a living reminder of ancient Hawai'i as any spot in the chain, the island is also sometimes known as the Separate Kingdom. Or the Unconquerable Island. Today, Kaua'i retains a feeling of separateness: Of the four main islands (the others being O'ahu, Maui and Hawai'i), Kaua'i—the eldest—has the smallest population.

Kaua'i did not come by its Separate Kingdom moniker easily. It was the only island able to withstand the forces of Kamehameha I as he swept through the rest of the chain in the late 1700s, conquering six of the other seven islands and uniting them under one monarch for the first time in Hawai'i's history. In part, the island was saved by its remoteness from the others—Kamehameha's first attempt at conquest, in 1796, was thwarted by a storm in the channel between O'ahu and Kaua'i. Eight years later, Kamehameha would try again, but the adverse effects of western contact would backhandedly benefit Kaua'i, when an illness—most likely cholera—decimated the attackers.

Though the saying goes "*Maui no ka 'oi*"—"Maui is number one"—Kaua'i is truly an island of firsts. Nearly 20 years before Kamehameha would attempt his Kaua'i attacks, Captain James Cook would make the first known landfall by a westerner in Hawai'i, anchoring the *Resolution* and *Discovery* on January 20, 1778, at Waimea, on Kaua'i's southwest coast.

In 1835, Ladd and Company leased a tract of land in the island's southeastern Kōloa area from Kamehameha III to grow cane—a crop that had been brought by Hawai'i's earliest groups of Polynesian settlers. Although the very first sugar in Hawai'i was produced in 1802 by Chinese immigrants on the island of Lāna'i, the sugar that would be produced at Kōloa was the first to be commercially exported from Hawai'i.

Later, the effects of this first export would be seen throughout the islands, as foreign (that is, American) sugar growers became increasingly influential in Hawaiian government—eventually becoming one of the driving forces behind the unlawful overthrow of Queen Lili'uokalani on O'ahu in 1893 and Hawai'i's subsequent annexation by the United States . . . and even, to a lesser extent, the push toward Statehood in 1959.

Pages 4-5: *Kalalau Valley on the Nā Pali Coast.*
Background: *Kalalau Beach and waterfall on the Nā Pali Coast.*
Above: *Hikers on the Kalalau Trail admiring the view of the Nā Pali Coast.*

These were the long-term effects of sugar. In the short term, the Kōloa plantation brought about other changes. In ancient times Wailua, on the island's east coast, was the religious capital of Kaua'i, while Waimea was the more secular capital. Once Kōloa started importing equipment for its mill and later exporting sugar, the tiny Kōloa Landing became the major port on the island—and would remain so for nearly a century. The town that sprung up around the mill became a major population center.

Like Lahaina on Maui and Honolulu on O'ahu, Kōloa was also affected (albeit briefly) by the whaling industry. Beginning circa 1830, peaking in the early 1840s and declining by 1860, the whaling industry further transported Kōloa Landing—to this day, some still refer to the area as "Whaler's Cove."

And of course, Kōloa's sugar plantations would have another effect still visible today. Like the rest of Hawai'i, the lack of labor necessary to grow and harvest cane meant that laborers and field managers were imported from across the globe. Today, one of the remotest spots in the Pacific Ocean is inhabited not only by Hawaiians but by second and third generation families from China, Japan, the Philippines, Portugal, Puerto Rico and throughout Europe.

Though spots like Wailua and Waimea had been inhabited for centuries, other towns on Kaua'i didn't even emerge until the early decades of the 19th century. Līhu'e, for example, is not referred to in any historical texts until 1837. Prior to that, the main trail from Waimea to Wailua bypassed the area completely, traveling inland instead. Sugar, however, would transform Līhu'e. When William Harrison Rice took over as manager of the Līhu'e Plantation in 1854, production was increased dramatically. Today, Līhu'e is located just outside the island's main airport and is the island's county seat.

Opposite: *The old plantation town of Koloa near Poʻipū Beach.* Above: *Alakoko Menehune Fish Pond near Nāwiliwili Harbor.*

Like all of Hawaiʻi, Kauaʻi is a mix of the modern and the timeless. Princeville's planned resort area on the island's north coast even features its own airport; and yet, near Nāwiliwili Harbor on the island's south-east shore, one can still see the Alekoko Fishpond, said to be built in times long forgotten by the legendary Menehune—a mysterious race of people who, according to popular legend, came out only at night, had prodigious strength and minimal height (supposedly standing in the two- to three-foot range).

In a way, this peculiar mix is the simplest way to understand a sense of Kauaʻi's magic. It lingers everywhere.

E komo mai: Welcome to Kauaʻi.

HĀNAU

BIRTH

According to the Kumulipo, the ancient 2,077-line genealogical chant that recounts the creation of the Hawaiian Islands, Pele the Fire Goddess was among the first to set foot on Kaua'i. When she left Kawiki Nui (an area some equate with Tahiti or Bora Bora) in search of a new home, the first large island she set foot on was Kaua'i. Unfortunately for her, every time she tried to dig a crater deep enough to store her fires, she struck sea water. The island turned out to be too small to house her flames and, pursued by a jealous sister intent on using the ocean to swamp her fires, she eventually made her way to her present, spacious living quarters in Halema'uma'u crater on the island of Hawai'i. This tale is still told throughout the Pacific to explain why Olokele, the volcano that formed the island, has long been extinct—while vents on the Big Island continue to spew lava to this day.

It is believed that Marquesans crossed some 2,000 miles of the Pacific Ocean to be the first humans to discover the Hawaiian Islands, somewhere around 500 A.D., and that their first settlements were established near 750 A.D.—quite possibly on Kaua'i. Because the island was settled so early in Hawai'i's history, and also perhaps because of its remoteness from the other islands in the chain, the royal bloodline of Kaua'i was considered by many to be the purest, and its chieftains were considered among the most sacred. Indeed, myth has it that Pele herself once fell in love with Lohi'au, a handsome and powerful Kaua'i chief.

Even before Pele made her mythic journey, Kaua'i would have long broken the surface of the Pacific Ocean. Though most people consider "Hawai'i" to consist merely of the eight major islands strung like a lei across a 400-mile area in the north Pacific, the Hawaiian island chain actually stretches some 1,600 miles and includes more than 130 islands, islets and atolls—most of which are uninhabited.

Whether one chooses to believe the mythic or scientific accounts, every island in the Hawaiian chain has a common origin. According to the Kumulipo, the islands were created by the union of Wākea the Sky-Father and Papa the Earth-Mother. The islands are literally children of the gods.

The more pragmatic explanation has it that every island, from the submerged Emperor Seamount on the extreme northwestern end of the chain to the island of Hawai'i on the far southeast end (and beyond to the still active, and submerged, Lō'ihi volcano), was formed by a single "hot spot" beneath the earth's crust. Over the course of millions of years, this hot spot has remained stationary, while the earth's crust has

Background : *New lava at Kamoamoa Black Sand Beach, Big Island.*
Above: *Glowing lava flow at night.*
Opposite: *Golden sunset over the Nā Pali Coast.*

Above: *Waimea Canyon*   Opposite: *Waterfall tumbling down from Mt. Wai'ale'ale.*

migrated to the northwest at approximately four inches per year, all the while opening new vents through which lava belched up to create the various islands in the chain. According to most estimates, the volcano that formed Kaua'i first began erupting some 10 million years ago; after rising nearly three miles, the lava broke the surface of the ocean several million years ago.

Today, the remnants of the volcano that formed Kaua'i make up the island's most dominant single feature: Mount Wai'ale'ale (which literally translates as "rippling waters"). For most of the year, Wai'ale'ale's 5,148-foot summit is shrouded in clouds—a state which led the island's earliest inhabitants to believe that the gods met beneath this misty cloak to determine

the fate of the islands. In a very real sense, Wai'ale'ale's hidden peaks do determine much of what happens on Kaua'i—this area receives an average of 460 inches of rainfall per year, making it the wettest spot on earth and feeding the rivers, waterfalls and lush vegetation of the island's lower reaches. (Like all islands, however, the rain can be localized. Areas a mere 20 miles away receive less than 20 inches of rain per year).

The once-fiery crater at the top of Wai'ale'ale is now the Alaka'i Swamp. Thirteen miles across and 30 square miles in total, Alaka'i is the largest high-elevation swamp in the world; its seven rivers trail out and down in all directions to the sea. One of these rivers, Waimea ("reddish water"), is the longest river in Hawai'i.

As the eldest of the major Hawaiian islands, Kaua'i's face has the deepest lines. On every side, one sees the effects of erosion at work: Olokele Volcano once pushed more than 10,000 feet into the heavens. Today, the mountain has been eroded down to two main peaks that were once a part of its eastern flank—Wai'ale'ale and Kawaikini (5,243 feet)—while the rest of the mountain sank and formed the crater which houses Alaka'i Swamp.

Waimea Canyon occupies 14 miles on the island's west end, its deep, rain-carved valleys and craggy spires giving ample credence to its nickname: The Grand Canyon of the Pacific. To the north, the Nā Pali Coast encompasses some 15 miles of nearly impassable terrain. Nā Pali, Hawaiian for "the cliffs," rises out of the sea to heights of over 3,000 feet—in many places making a sheer vertical drop to the sea. At approximately the same time that Kaua'i broke the surface, the island of Ni'ihau rose up 17.2 miles away across a shallow ocean channel (some speculate that the island was actually a part of Kaua'i at one time).

After millenia of erosion, Kaua'i has reached its present state—33 miles long and 25 miles wide at its widest points, with an area of 627 miles (and 90 miles of coastline). Today, the island can essentially be divided into four geographic areas: the north coast, running roughly from Hā'ena through Hanalei and Princeville to Kīlauea; the east coast, which encompasses the areas of Anahola, Kapa'a and Wailua; the south coast, from Līhu'e through Kōloa, Hanapēpē, Waimea town and out to the end of Highway 50 at Mānā; and the west and northwest coasts are dominated by the dual wonders of Waimea Canyon and the Nā Pali Coast. (Kaua'i's "Belt Highway" is actually a broken chain. No road has been built to span the undulating grandeur of the Nā Pali coastline).

Born 10 million years ago, it isn't hard to see why Kaua'i is still something of a child—that is, a child of the gods.

Honopū Beach on the Nā Pali Coast.

FOOD OF THE GODS

KALO AND HANALEI VALLEY

BEFORE THERE WERE HUMANS, there was *kalo* (more commonly, if mistakenly, known as taro). Like Kaua'i itself, the starchy root is literally born of the gods: Wākea the Sky-Father and Papa the Earth-Mother created a beautiful daughter named Ho'ohōkū-kalani. Wākea could not resist the beauty of his own daughter, and they were united; Ho'ohōkūkalani would eventually deliver a stillborn child out of this union. From the child's grave sprouted the first *kalo* plant. Wākea would call this child Hāloa-naka, in reference to the *kalo* plant's long (*hāloa*) and quivering (*naka*) leaves. Thus, according to the Hawaiian cosmology, *kalo* comes even before humans in the hierarchy of the universe.

Later, Wākea and Ho'ohōkūka-lani would have a second child, whom they would name Hāloa in honor of the *kalo* which nourished him in his youth. *Kalo* thus became a staple food of the Hawaiian people, who consider the plant to be their ancestor Hāloa—the plant's heart-shaped leaves and edible root directly linking them to the land beneath their feet and the gods above.

Today Hanalei Valley, on Kaua'i's north coast, produces 60 percent of all the *kalo* grown for poi in the Islands. Cultivated in knee-deep water, on terraced steps of land known as *lo'i*, it's not surprising that Hanalei would be an ideal spot for the plant. The rivers

flowing out of Alaka'i Swamp and into the valley provide a constant supply of water.

At one time, archeologists believe, Hanalei Valley fed and supported tens of thousands of native Hawaiians. One thing is certain: for centuries, the valley was used almost exclusively for the production of *kalo* (many of the original terraced fields can still be made out). However, western contact changed all of this. Not only did diseases carried by foreigners decimate the native population, but foreign plantings would for many years supplant *kalo* as the native crop.

Once westerners arrived, a number of other crops were experimented with. Coffee and cane both eventually failed. Cattle were brought in, denuding the land through overgrazing. By this time, Hanalei actually had to import poi from further north, in neighboring Kalalau. Chinese laborers moving into the valley near the turn of the 20th century re-established the terraces of Hanalei, but this time to plant rice—a crop which would be grown well into the 1930s. In the end, thankfully, *kalo* prevailed. Yet, even with Hanalei back to producing the majority of the poi consumed in the Islands, it is not uncommon for this staple—at family gatherings and tourist lū'au—to be rationed. Often, in stores across the island chain, one sees a familiar sign: "Sorry, out of poi."

Background: *Taro or "kalo" harvest in Hanalei Valley.*
Above: *Taro field in the afternoon light, Hanalei Valley.*

Opposite page: *Harvesting the Taro root, Hanalei Valley.*
Right: *Smiling face of Eve Koga harvesting taro.* Below: *Hanalei Valley taro field.*
Pages 20-21: *Early morning over peaceful Hanalei Valley.*

NORTH COAST

FROM KĪLAUEA TO KĒ'Ē BAY

ESSENTIALLY, THE NORTH COAST OF KAUA'I begins with Kīlauea. The lighthouse that stands sentinel here is a gateway to the rest of the coast, as well as a still functioning beacon for ships passing through the occasionally huge winter swells that bear down on Hawai'i from the Aleutian Islands in Alaska. Built in 1913, the lighthouse is designated a national historic landmark, and boasts the world's largest "clamshell" lens—a lens capable of creating a light bright enough to be seen 90 miles from shore. (The clamshell lens, however, has not been used since the mid-'70s, having been replaced by a much smaller light).

For those willing to search a little, the Kīlauea area is also home to some fine beaches. Though most of the access roads are unmarked and the best of the beaches can only be found through the help of someone familiar with the area, those lucky enough to find their way to Kauapea (a.k.a. Secret Beach), Kalihiwai Bay or Anini Beach will marvel at their beauty—and, for the most part, lack of crowds.

Traveling further northeast on Highway 56 leads to Princeville—its 11,000 acres of planned resort community a startling contrast to the more rural aspects of the surrounding environs. Named after Prince Albert, the son of King Kamehameha IV and Queen Emma

(who once summered here), the area was once a huge ranch owned by a Scotsman named R. C. Wyllie. Today, Princeville is home to its own airport, fire and police departments. It also stands sentinel over one of the most beautiful sites on earth—Hanalei ("crescent bay").

Walled in by *pali* that sometimes reach as high as 3,500 feet, Hanalei valley is the definition of *impressive*. Numerous waterfalls tumble over the cliff edge to feed Hanalei River, which works its way through the center of the stepped valley, down to the wide flat beach and into the sea.

Though tiny Hanalei town passes by in the snap of a finger, those who stop for a look won't be disappointed—in part because the town is situated near one of the most beautiful bays in all of Hawai'i. Known as one of the Pacific's most perfect anchorages since the times of the early Polynesians, Hanalei Bay is still a prime spot for visiting yachts—at least, during the summer months. In the winter, when large waves wash in powered by the Aleutian storms, the bay can be treacherous. In the summer and fall months, visitors might see the tiny Hanalei Canoe Club practicing in the bay—tiny but powerful, that is. HCC has firmly established itself as one of the strongest outrigger clubs in the Islands.

Background: *Kalihiwai Bay looking toward the Kīlauea area.*
Above: *The Kīlauea Lighthouse.*

Above: *Peaceful countryside in the Kīlauea area.* Below, left to right: *Looking out to Kīlauea Point and Kīlauea Lighthouse. Historic Wai'oli Church, Hanalei.*
Opposite, top to bottom: *Golfers on the Prince Course, Princeville Resort. Pu'u Pōā Beach at Princeville.*

Opposite, top to bottom and left to right: *People relaxing in the central area of Hanalei. Road into Hanalei. Looking toward the center of Hanalei. Puʻu Pōā Beach at Princeville. Quiet moments in Hanalei.*

Above: *Summer afternoon, Hanalei Bay. Rainbows over Hanalei Valley.* Left: *Wind surfing near Hāʻena Beach.* Right: *Ching Young Store, Hanalei.* Pages 28-29: *Sunset over Hanalei Bay*

This page, left to right and top to bottom: Aerial of coastal road in the Lumaha'i area. Overview of Hā'ena area. The Wainiha General Store. One lane bridge over the Wainiha River. Early morning at "Y Camp Beach" near Hā'ena.
Opposite: Lumaha'i Beach.

Above: *Lone snorkeler gliding through pristine waters below Princeville. Limahuli Stream in Limahuli Valley, Hā'ena area.*
Opposite: *Taro or "Kalo" terraces at Limahuli Gardens, one of the National Tropical Botanical Gardens.*

Six miles down the road, the pavement ends at Kē'ē Bay—itself one of the most historic sites in Hawai'i. Not only does this area mark the beginning of the 11-mile hiking trail into Nā Pali's Kalalau Valley, but it is also home to the legendary birthplace of hula—Kauluapa'oa Heiau. Standing on a bluff overlooking the offshore Lehua Island, it isn't hard to see why this area is thought to be the inspiration for Hawai'i's famed dance. Like the hula, the view from Kauluapa'oa is breathtaking.

Opposite, left to right and top to bottom: *Sunset at Kē'ē Beach. Hikers descending the Kalalau Trail above Kē'ē Beach. Kayakers headed out to sea from Kē'ē Beach.* Above: *Ka'ula Paoa Heiau above Kē'ē Beach.* Right: *Strolling along Kē'ē Beach at sunset.*

THE TOWN THAT CANE BUILT

LĪHUʻE: JUMPING OFF POINT

UNLESS ONE IS DARING ENOUGH TO RISK the 60-mile ocean crossing between Oʻahu and Kauaʻi, or is wealthy enough to fly into Princeville's exclusive airport, most travelers enter and leave Kauaʻi through Līhuʻe—the county seat and population center of the island (with a whopping 4,000 residents). Though not the center of the island, Līhuʻe is nonetheless centrally located, being roughly midway between Hāʻena at the northern end of Kauaʻi's so-called Belt Highway and Mānā point on the highway's western end.

Interestingly, this central location barely existed before the advent of sugar in Hawaiʻi. Though the town was founded in the early 1800s, it remained little more than a sleepy backwater before cane came along. Even then, neighboring Kōloa, the oldest plantation in Hawaiʻi, was for a time the major force in Kauaʻi's sugar industry. This was to change due to the vision of Henry A. Peirce, who saw Līhuʻe's future rooted in sugar. In 1849 Peirce convinced two friends, William L. Lee (Chief Justice of the Supreme Court of Hawaiʻi) and Charles R. Bishop (who would later found Hawaiʻi's first permanent bank) to put up half of the $16,000 in start-up funds for H.A.

Peirce & Co. This money was to transform not only Līhuʻe, but the process of growing cane in general—in part because $1,000 per year of it (an exceptional wage for the times) was used to hire James Marshall, who introduced irrigation to Hawaiʻi.

While Marshall proved to be a well-suited manager, there may have been another, more practical reason for his original hiring. In 1843, the English naval captain Lord George Paulet attempted to forcefully annex Hawaiʻi in the name of England. It was Marshall who traveled to both Washington and London with secret dispatches on the matter, acquainting both the United States and England with the situation and heading off a potential overthrow of the Hawaiian monarchy. The Hawaiian Crown thus owed a debt of gratitude to Marshall, which may have in part been paid off by granting Peirce and Co. access to between 2,000 and 3,000 acres of land above Līhuʻe town.

At any rate, credit is due to Henry Peirce for making Līhuʻe what it is today—a jumping off point to explore the rest of Kauaʻi, and an historic reminder of sugar cane's once dominant and all-encompassing hold on Hawaiʻi.

Pages 36-37: *Sunset and waves looking toward the Nā Pali Coast.*
Background: *The downtown area and main street of Līhuʻe.*
Above: *Local resident at orchid sale, the Kauaʻi Museum.*

WAILUA NUI HOʻĀNO

WAILUA AND THE EAST COAST

THOUGH STRUNG WITH BEAUTIFUL BEACHES like Anahola Bay (not far eastward of Kīlauea), the true gem of Kauaʻi's east coast is Wailua. The first arrival of Polynesians in Hawaiʻi is believed to have occurred at the mouth of the Wailua River. In ancient times, this was the spiritual center of the island—a fact that is still visible in the numerous ruins of *heiau* (temples) scattered throughout the area. Here, near Lydgate State Park, the unique Hikina a ka Lā (*rising of the sun*) heiau can be found. A mere 56 feet wide and 395 feet long, the heiau stretches due north, in an orientation with the North Star. It was also built on the spot in Wailua where the rays of the sun first touch in the morning. Estimated to have been built sometime shortly after the arrival of the first Marquesans in approximately 800 A.D., it is one of the oldest heiau in the Islands. Within walking distance of Hikina a ka Lā are a number of petroglyph-covered stones, and at least two other major heiau.

In ancient times, Wailua was the gateway to one of the most powerful spots in the Islands. Atop Waiʻaleʻale sits a small plateau, in the middle of which sits a pond that gives the mountain its name—"Rippling on the Water." This spot was the site of a major altar to the god Kāne, who is the god of living creatures, the spirit of the water and the lord of the forests. It is Kāne who remains hidden under Waiʻaleʻale's clouds.

To reach this site, chiefs and priests most likely traveled up the Wailua River, by canoe to begin with, and then on foot toward the summit—following the course of the river up through Wailua Valley, passing through stands of koa wood (used for making canoes) and sandalwood. Then they hiked up higher, into groves of the storied ōhiʻa-lehua tree. (Ōhiʻa and Lehua were lovers separated by Pele's jealousy. Hiʻiaka, a sister of Pele, took pity on the pair, turning them into a tree so that they might be forever united. This, it is said, is why one shouldn't pick the tree's beautiful lehua blossoms—if the lovers are separated, it will rain tears from heaven.)

The famed Menehune, builders of heiau and other ancient sites, were active in Wailua in other ways as well. Not far from the river, if one glances up toward the mountain skyline, the outline of the Sleeping Giant becomes clear. It's said that he's been there since the point in time when the Menehune first tried to waken him by throwing stones. So many stones landed in the giant's mouth that he eventually came down with an incurable case of indigestion — and so remains sleeping to this day.

Today, the Wailua River has become the site of a different kind of pilgrimage. From a small landing, boatloads of tourists travel up the river daily to the Fern Grotto—a gigantic old lava tube draped in ferns, set back into the rainforest. While chiefs once traveled

Background: *Lush greenery surrounding a tour boat on the Wailua River.*
Above: *Heiau in Lydgate Park, Wailua River area.*

this river on their way to worship a god, visitors today travel the same path for a different sort of ceremony—the Fern Grotto is one of the most popular spots in the Islands for a wedding ceremony.

Whether chieftain, kahuna (priest) or newlywed, it isn't hard to see why Wailua would hold such a powerful attraction . . . nor why, in older times, the portion of Wailua that borders the bay was referred to as Wailua Nui Ho'āno—Great Sacred Wailua. So powerful is this area that it is revered not only in Hawaiian legend, but also turns up in tales of certain parts of Central Polynesia.

Left: Sunday services at the Ana-hola Baptist Church. Below: Anahola Beach on the northeast-ern shore.

Opposite: Lū'aū preparation in the imu (underground oven) in Waipouli.

Left: *The Kapaʻa coastline on the Eastern shoreline. The Sleeping Giant above Kapaʻa.*

Right, top to bottom: *The town of Kapaʻa looking out to the Sleeping Giant. An art gallery in Kapaʻa. The Kauaʻi Village Market and Museum in Waipouli.*

Clockwise from top left: *Wailua Falls. Fisherman throwing a net out to sea. A tour boat on the Wailua River. The Fern Grotto. Coconut Grove in Waipouli. Opposite, clockwise from top left: 'Ōpaeka'a Falls. The Lydgate Park area near Wailua. Poli'ahu Heiau. River boat on the Wailua River. Ancient burial ground (heiau) in Lydgate State Park. Visitors at Poli'ahu Heiau in Wailua River State Park.*

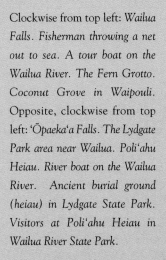

THE LITTLE PEOPLE?

THE MENEHUNE

THROUGHOUT HAWAI'I, and especially on Kaua'i, one will often come across ancient sites of mysterious origin. Most often, these sites—heiau, fishponds, dams and other constructions—are attributed to Menehune.

Over the years, Menehune have become increasingly mythologized and, it appears, westernized. The popular perception of the Menehune is that they were a race of little people, not unlike leprechauns. Very shy, they purportedly only worked at night—either completing all work in the course of one evening or forever abandoning the site. Despite their limited size, Menehune were believed to have prodigious strength.

All of which makes for a good legend, but it seems that very little is based in fact. And in this case, fact is more interesting than fiction. When the first census was taken on Kaua'i, in 1820, a group of 65 natives living in the upper Wainiha Valley—on the island's northern coast—identified themselves as Menehune.

The earliest Hawaiian legends about Menehune make no mention of their lesser stature, though they are referred to as being of a lower *status*. More than one researcher has thus hypothesized that the Menehune might in fact be the original Marquesan settlers—this because the Marquesans were eventually subjugated by later waves of Tahitians, circa 1200 A.D. This would make sense given, as some point out, the fact that the Tahitian word *manahune* refers to one of lower status. It is not unlikely that the Marquesans were not only driven into the forests by the more powerful Tahitians, but also that they were put to work as stonemasons and laborers by their conquerors.

Whatever the truth about the Menehune, some of the most ancient and famous sites on Kaua'i are today attributed to their skilled hands. Among the best known of these is the Alekoko Fishpond, near Lihu'e. Used as an early form of aquaculture, Hawaiian fishponds essentially dam off a part of a river or bay, allowing water and young fish to enter through small gaps, but trapping larger fish for harvest as needed. In the case of Alekoko, a wall some 900 feet in length cuts off a bend in the river that flows into Nāwili-wili Harbor. Five feet above the water level and four feet wide on top, legend has it that every stone was passed hand-to-hand between a double row of Menehune from a quarry site in Makaweli—some 25 miles away. Whatever the true origins of the Menehune, it's clear that they were a race of incredible skill and, it would appear, supernatural strength.

Background: *Alekoko Menehune Fishpond.*
Above: *Ancient Valley showing Kalo Lo'i, sometimes said to have been built by the Menehune.*

WELCOME TO RUSSIA?

SOUTH AND WEST KAUA'I

WHEN SPEAKING OF RUINS IN HAWAI'I, most tend to think of traditional religious or agricultural sites—areas that hold keys to Hawai'i's ancient past. On Kaua'i, however, there is also debris of a more recent vintage. Fort Elizabeth, for instance, stands as a remnant of the days when powers besides the United States were jockeying for position in the strategically located Hawaiian Islands.

In the early 1800s, a Russian agent named Anton Scheffer arrived on Kaua'i and went to work gaining the graces of the ruling chief, Kaumuali'i. At this point, Kaumuali'i—realizing that it was only a matter of time before Kamehameha would overcome a string of ill fate to put together a successful invasion of Kaua'i—had already somewhat reluctantly pledged his allegiance to the warrior king on O'ahu. Knowing this, Scheffer promised the chief independence from Kamehameha. In return, Kaumuali'i allowed Scheffer to build a fort overlooking Waimea Bay. Shaped like a 6-pointed star and named after the daughter of Czar Nicholas, the Russian flag was first raised over Scheffer's fort in 1817.

Scheffer, being a somewhat enterprising operator, would eventually build other forts in Honolulu and along the Wai'oli River, above Hanalei Bay. Though he made his way into Kaua'i's seats of power, Scheffer was never truly able to win the trust of Czar Nicholas, who eventually withdrew official support—and Kaumuali'i would eventually drive Scheffer out of Hawai'i. Even so, Kaumuali'i continued to fly the Russian flag over the fort for quite some time. The fort would eventually be stripped of its guns and for the most part dismantled in 1864.

It is not surprising that Scheffer would choose Waimea as the site of his first stronghold, since the bay was one of the main anchorages in Kaua'i and throughout the Islands. It was here that Captain James Cook first landed in Hawai'i, having made his "discovery" official by coming ashore at 3:30 p.m. on September 20, 1778.

Waimea, however, is only one small piece of Kaua'i's southwest coast. Leaving Lihu'e and heading west along Highway 50, one first passes through Puhi—home of Kaua'i Community College—and by the Maluhia Road, which branches off toward Kōloa and is famed for its tunneling passage through groves of eucalyptus.

Further along is Po'ipū Beach, well known as a resort destination and one of the finer beaches on the island. Then come the ex-sugar towns: Kalāheo (the site of a generous gift of land by the philanthropist Walter McBride, which would eventually become Kukui 'O Lono Park); Hanapēpē and Olokele. They all point to King Sugar's past dominance on the island.

Each town is unique; each historic—whether it be in terms of an ancient past or as reminders of all that has occurred to make Kaua'i the island that it is today.

Background: *Surf and jagged rocks on the Po'ipū coastline at Keoniloa Bay.*
Above: *The Russian Fort or Fort Elizabeth at Waimea.*

Clockwise from top left: *Poʻipū Beach scenes — The tree tunnel and road to the beach. Snorkeling. Hawaiian Monk Seal. Hyatt Regency pool. Looking out toward the ocean. Opposite, top to bottom and left to right: Poʻipū Beach Park. Golf tournament at Poʻipū Bay Resort. 16th fairway, Poʻipū Bay Resort. Overlooking Kalāheo. Kukuiʻula Bay and Harbor.*
Pages 54-55: Spouting Horn.

Opposite, top to bottom and left to right: *Hanapēpē storefront. Old truck alongside the road in Hanapēpē. Above coffee plantations and Hanapēpē Canyon looking toward 'Ele'ele and Hanapēpē. The statue of James Cook in Waimea. The town of Waimea.* Above: *Hanapēpē.* Left: *Small church in the sugarcane fields, Makaweli.* Right: *The Waimea Plantation Cottages and grove of palm trees.* Below: *The statue of James Cook.*

Above: *Looking toward Niʻihau and Lehua.* Left: *Team spirit in Kekaha.* Right: *Polihale Beach.* Below, left to right: *Riding horses in Kekaha. Plantation town of Kekaha. Bonfire on Kekaha Beach. Couple in the surf off Kekaha with Niʻihau beyond.*

GRAND CANYON OF THE PACIFIC

WAIMEA CANYON AND NĀ PALI COAST

THE LAST VOLCANIC ERUPTION ON KAUA'I took place an estimated 1.5 million years ago. Since then, the effects of erosion have been working a slow and patient transformation of the island's landscape. By far, the most dramatic results of these eons of weathering are to be found on the western and northwestern portions of the island—at Waimea Canyon and along the Nā Pali Coast.

Nearly 3,000 feet deep and 14 miles across, Waimea Canyon is truly phenomenal—and if not for Kōke'e Road and Waimea Canyon Drive, the area would be all but inaccessible by land to any but the hardiest travelers. But there is a road, and the drive is like no other in the world. Winding up either Waimea Canyon Drive from Waimea town or Kōke'e Road from Kekaha, the coastal towns drop down and away, merging into a series of alternating emerald green and pale blue vistas, as the view trades off between layers of cultivated fields and the ocean beyond.

Nearing the 2,000-foot level, the landscape changes immensely—fields give way to gnarled trees that cling to the bare, red earth. By the time one reaches the Waimea Canyon Overlook, at 3,400 feet, nearly all of the canyon is visible—as are high-flying birds, mountain goats and the occasional low-flying tour heli-

copter. Further on, at the Pu'u Kapele Lookout, the Waipo'o Waterfall comes into view, tumbling down a steep valley further up the canyon. Once at Pu'u Hinahina Lookout, the view turns spectacularly downward toward the sea.

Beyond Pu'u Hinahina lies the Kōke'e State Park. From here the road leads to one of the most spectacular views in the world—the Kalalau Lookout, which overlooks the northwestern end of Nā Pali's 15-mile stretch of coastline. With its towering cliff faces rising to heights of over 3,500 feet from the crashing seas below, this coast would appear to be uninhabitable—but this is only true when looking at the area through modern eyes. Kalalau Valley, remote and beautiful, was once the home to a thriving agricultural community—albeit one that lived in a fair amount of isolation.

Archeological digs along the Nā Pali Coast yield a good deal of evidence that the area was once a thriving community. Carved fish-hooks, stone tools, files made of coral and hand drills with bone and stone drill-bits all point to a well-developed community living in what we would now—with our backward sense of the word—consider to be isolation.

Indeed, Kalalau, one of the places furthest removed

Background: *Hikers on the rim of Waimea Canyon.*
Above: *Waimea Canyon.*

Above: *Along the road to Kōkeʻe and Waimea Canyon. Right: The Iliau plant along the rim of* Waimea Canyon. Below: Contours of Waimea Canyon.

from Kaua'i's currently inhabited areas, was once home to a sizable population and was extensively terraced and irrigated along its four-mile floor. Even more isolated was Kalalau's western neighbor, Nu'alolo Kai Valley. So inaccessible was the valley that the only way in and out was via rope ladders hanging from the cliff faces. Yet even today, the remnants of a remarkably sophisticated series of *kalo lo'i* are easily made out.

Opposite: *Enjoying the view of Kalalau Valley (top). Brunch along the rim of Kalalau Valley (bottom).* This page, left, top to bottom: *Hikers on the Pihea Trail. The 'Ōhi'a Lehua blossom. Kalalau Valley and waterfall. Hawai'i's state bird, the nēnē. A mountain cabin in Kōke'e.* Above: *The Kōke'e Museum.*

Unlike the other islands, Hawaiians moved far inland in this area, exchanging the more usual sea-going staple foods for agricultural harvests.

Standing atop the Kalalau Lookout and gazing to the east, it is hard to imagine the forces that created this coastline, or that it could ever have been anything other than the jagged series of cliffs that it now is. For years the theory was that this coast was formed strictly through the erosive effects of wind and rain and the powerful northern ocean swells that batter the area in the winter.

Only relatively recently has a different model been proposed for the creation of this natural wonder. In 1964, a geologist by the name of James G. Moore broke from conventional geological theory, suggesting that

Pages 66-67: *Kalalau Valley.*
This page: *Scenes along the Nā Pali Coast: a pink kayak, a tour catamaran, a sailboat and a tour boat.* Opposite, top and bottom: *Two scenes along the Nā Pali Coast.*

much of Nā Pali's dizzying coastline was not formed over millions of years but extremely quickly. It was Moore's hypothesis that cliff faces like Nā Pali on Kaua'i and O'ahu's Nu'uanu Pali are actually the result of landslides—extremely large landslides. In the case of Nā Pali, a 62-mile-wide avalanche scooped away a huge part of the island some 5 million years ago, depositing material some 87 miles off shore. Another smaller landslide (about half the size) would later scoop away parts of the island's southern coast.

Sound impossible? Many thought so, until quite recently. If not for—of all people—then U.S. president Ronald Reagan, this would all still probably be written off as rather outlandish conjecture. But it was Reagan who, in 1983, declared U.S. sovereignty over all resources within a 230-mile U.S. Exclusive Economic Zone, which extended offshore from all U.S. territories—Hawai'i included. When the U.S. Geological Survey set out to map this new territory, a startling discovery was made. Sonar mapping showed that there had been 68 major landslides (each more than 12 miles in length) on islands throughout the 1,600-mile

island chain. Giant avalanches deposited debris as far as 53 miles off the coast of Maui in one instance; in another, stone slabs more than six miles across tumbled as far as 30 miles offshore of O'ahu.

Standing at the Kalalau Lookout and trying to imagine a 60-mile piece of land simply dropping into the sea is almost too much for the mind to grasp. Suddenly, the view becomes all the more stunning—and nearly unbelievable.

Pages 70-71: *The twin beaches of Honopū, Nā Pali Coast.*
Opposite, top to bottom: *Kalalau Beach. One of the twin beaches at Honopū. Waterfall flowing into the Waimea River.* Above: *Golden afternoon light over the cliffs of the Nā Pali Coast.* Right: *The jagged cliffs and Mt. Waiʻaleʻale.*

KAUA'I KILOHANA

FROM KALALAU'S ancient and abandoned *kalo* fields to Līhu'e's once thriving cane plantations; from Waimea Canyon's vast desolation to Princeville's bustling exclusivity—Kaua'i is a land of multiple faces, both literally and figuratively. Barely 60 miles from O'ahu's crowded streets, to this day the island stands as a land apart. An unconquerable island and a separate kingdom.

Whether overlooking Nā Pali's immense grandeur, the magical wonder of the Alekoko Fishpond with its mysterious origins, or even sipping a Mai Tai at one of the island's famed resorts as the sun sets, it is no exaggeration to say that this is a land of magic—an island born of the gods. It is no wonder that ancient Hawaiians sometimes called it *Kaua'i kilohana*, for it is exactly that: Superior Kaua'i.

Clockwise from top left: *Looking toward Hanalei Bay from Princeville. Sunset over Kalalau Valley.*
Girl on beach with pink umbrella. Island girl.
Opposite: *Silhouette of a kahiko hula dancer at sunset. Inset: Kalāheo youngsters.*
Page 76: *Sunset at the Spouting Horn in Po'ipū (top).*
Fisherman at the end of the day at Kē'ē Beach, Hā'ena (bottom).